THE WISHBONE DRESS

WINNER OF THE 2019 FROST PLACE
CHAPBOOK COMPETITION

THE WISHBONE DRESS

POEMS

Cassandra J. Bruner

DURHAM, NORTH CAROLINA

The Wishbone Dress

Winner of the 2019 *Frost Place Chapbook Competition*
Selected by Eduardo C. Corral

Copyright ©2019 by Cassandra J. Bruner.

All rights reserved. No part of this book may be reproduced, scanned, or distributed in any printed or electronic form without permission.

Library of Congress Cataloging-in-Publication Data
Bruner, Cassandra J.
The Wishbone Dress: poems / by Cassandra J. Bruner
p. cm.
ISBN-13: 978-1-949344-09-7

Published in the United States of America
Book design by Spock and Associates

Cover photograph by Jennifer Thoreson
Flora 1, from the series *Flora*, 2010
www.jenniferthoreson.com

Published by
BULL CITY PRESS
1217 Odyssey Drive
Durham, NC 27713

www.BullCityPress.com

CONTENTS

FRONTISPIECE

I think of how gods prefer their oracles
blind & their prophets impotent,

how two milligrams of estrogen
was enough to mold Eve from a shard of bone.

If only the world would hush,
I could hear my skin thinning.

Listen: sleep is a wasp's nest inside the mouth.
Come morning, I am doubled over

the sink, spitting stingers & wings. Each heave
a prayer for a homeland,

a recitation of the Song of Songs.
In this manner, the body learns its shape.

As I scrub the lining of my cheeks
with lemons,

the rinds speak
in my great-grandmother's voice—

Child, your hips have already fused.
A gash in my mouth sings

of all things made new
as it hardens like a cataract.

AUBADE WITH BALL GAG

> *"Masturbathon" is the ideal form of sex activity for this trans-gendered subject.*
> -Slavoj Žižek

Love   in this omnivorous air
this weave of straps & copper   we must look like
a lone woman   who can't stop
touching herself

A tangled braid
of bone   A prairie of orchids
speckled in amber   in pudendum
in hooks   Please   lean

closer   & hear the cries crackle
along my jaw like hooves   The spit
circle my throat   like a supplicant

Before re-entering the world that makes
a husband of me   you clench
the absence of my breasts

At the unclasping   our twinned watermark
our afterimage   fading

THE ANTLERED DOE

A man doused in roebuck piss says
I saw it as I skinned its thighs
& laughs.

Your death always a joke, the shock
of womb, a punchline.
Darting through

underbrush, your hooves
resounded like cackling children.
This velvet crown, not always a betrayal—

In rutting season, the tongues
of stags & doe alike climbed
your hind leg, crying
I opened for my beloved but she was gone.

Now is the hour of moths
& the body remade as
a sack of buckshot.

A child bundles you in sweat-stale
flannel, lifting you onto the truck bed
like a distant sister. Nestled

against your snout, he mouths
a wish for recognition, for his budding breasts
to hide themselves away like fawns.

CORA, BOUND TO THE TREE, DELIVERS HER TESTIMONY

Yes, your darkest fables

walk upright. My child was born limp & fevered
as a chewed-off tongue. Born hooved, horse-headed,
ridged with salmon scales, & choking on

his mane of kelp. The house moaned with the grief
I couldn't vocalize. Through twilight, I pried
with spoons & trowels at the groaning baseboards. They

split & I found a dried butterfly's tongue, a pile
of overripe oranges, a book shellacked with
the still-clicking beaks of hummingbirds—

Not everyone is so fortunate, to have their future plainly
spread before them. I dipped the proboscis in ink.
I scrawled my name into the singing ledger. I baptized

myself in those fruits' fermented juices. When an infant
crawled toward me—iridescent as oil on seawater
& furred with smog, but otherwise human—

I knew I had saved my child. What choice did I have then,
but to call the nearest shadow *Master* & tongue honey
from her calves? You, too, have whispered this forbidden

wish. This is why you now nail a drowned adolescent's
corpse to my doorstep, wreck my body with his accident,
its unspoken call for accusation. Let's enumerate my crimes—

I burned the beautyberries ringing your apiaries,
                warding off the teeming locusts & killer wasps.
When your husbands bore tumors shaped like God's

                swollen scrotum, I lanced & cleaned the seeping
wounds. In the summer of floods, I delivered
                newborns with prehensile tails & eyes veiled

by whalebaleen. Each mother I advised to hide yet cherish
                the blasphemy they bled for. To conceal gills beneath
brooches & collars, then stroke them lightly with lavender

                water. In short: I nourished my torturers better
than the son who delighted in gurgling my name. Go
                ahead. Puncture my ankles with an iron rod & call them

pillars of onyx when they refuse to shatter. Watch my
                hair flash into steel ribbons under your blades.
Make a profane miracle of me—

                When I burn, marbled crayfish will swarm the shore.
When I become smoke, a stainglass Joan of Arc
                will march the town square, allowing doubters

to finger her charred tissue. Torch me, & I'll return
                as seaweed & the clutch of skate eggs it cradles—
those brackish jewels a child might dive after, only

                to dissolve into the horizon of his name.

SWANPLUME BOY'S EPITHALAMIUM

Wanting the down, the purple, the blood of me dazzled & swelling,
you bite costume rubies into my hips. Nebula,
full-bloom. We wake to

coronas scratched
across lids, flanks, ribs. The spirit

rising into welt, as water expands &
crowns into ice.

Am I lake & drain & plug enough
for you? Pull

this strap-on, this
tucking, this harness till I unravel—
Seven shades of red. Flush & sinew. Teething moon,

can you hear the drowned hound moaning
under my collarbone? Can you

hear the skin cry,
Night, graft me
to you?

Say you're a carnivore. Say you'll
wound where I want. Say

your love, too, lashes itself to a flooding barn & inhales
those searing, those bursting
blues.

OF THE NIGHT

I wanted to joke about Moses loving god
having seen only his backside,
but friend, it's too early for sacrilege.
Instead, let's talk about whores.

Talk about my mother's devotional, *Bad Women of the Bible*,
which had her convinced local streetwalkers
wove nightgowns out of shadow & stripped
passersby with a flick of an eyelash.

Tracing makeshift lineages of harlotry, the book says
Azazel set apart the first whores when
he gifted us knives & make-up. Or pagan gods
forged us out of strawberry paste & fishnets. Or
we evolved from screech owls as bird-footed humans.

The author ultimately names Lilith foremother of whores,
inventor of the strap-on. See, she wanted Adam
to be a switch, making her wicked in the voyeuristic
eyes of the Lord.

For this desire, satyrs, night terrors,
& wet dreams would spill from her labia for millennia.
Because, by His will, a womb must always
give birth to something.

                    //

These histories scrape behind me
like a wedding train
as I skype Ann about stints of sex work.

Her Siberian Husky rests his snout in her lap,
licks salt from her fingertips, & I think
of Jezebel & the rabid hounds. How they left her palms
unchewed on the blood-soaked terrace,
as if they knew what kindness may have resided there.

Ann recalls how quickly a client's
sweetheart became *cunt*
as he brushed her orchiectomy scars, & I consider how
judgment is woven into flesh.

Like the time I undressed before a woman who
said *why the fuck didn't you tell me you have AIDS*
upon seeing my sore-peppered thighs.
Instead of explaining Crohn's—

its emaciations & abscesses, its fistulas & swelling,
its bleed & bloat—
I slid my leggings back on,
walked out.

                //

Someone once curved beneath
Ann like an uninvited guest, said
I've never felt safer as they untangled. Is
desire always defined by its negation, its absence?

Name us a god who is a hooker, whose laws are
be fluid & multiple, nourish one another
within reason—
We will kneel, unfurling
our perfumed nests of hair in offering.

WHEN I DEFEND MY NAME IN COURT

I arrive   smeared with filth
& crushed
asters   Palm pressed
to a leather bible   I say
my goddess is a nest of grime   my worship
a cheap strap-on   pursed under the tongue
The jury of gleaming women staple my birth
certificate to my forehead   reciting
the deadname while   by hand or
by vise   witnesses
fail to pry my hips wider   Without
verdict   the judge recounts
stories of women hexed
by the sun's spit   of women never
believed   Locked out
on the courthouse steps   my love
watches   transfixed   as a shrike
pins robin hearts to her left index   For want
of relief   for want of a branch

POEM OF MY SHAME

after Erika L. Sánchez's "Poem of My Humiliations"

Once, I cupped a robin's egg & it slipped from my palms, slick with sweat
      & dazzled by tremors.

Like they did when I slept with a woman who spat my name like an epithet.

She marked my imperfections with bird tags—

The undeveloped breasts. The pockets of cellulite. The pelvis gone
      soft with estrogen.

I lay still through each pinch of those plastic bands.

How often I've mistaken heat for light, for nourishment.

How often I've flinched from your embrace—

You, who watch me make meals of my longing until clothes hang loose
      from my ribs.

Friend, I know I've worn this disgrace like a wedding dress.

I've let goats lick the garter.

But understand, I remember the moments before she wound those
      blue ribbons of humiliation,

remember we were both smiling as we suspended our shirts above our heads, like
      a wreath of molted feathers.

Like a judgment.

PRAYER: SYRINX

I've had enough of gods   of dipping lips
to pondwater & receiving soundless ripples
in response   Let this psalm call to my body
instead   How she stiffened in his arms
Became phloem then marrow then phloem
again   A field salting itself before being
plucked fallow   How   pinned beneath
him   she witnessed the hoopoe stalk
a pair of nightingales   The hawk lance
voles on its talons   The thrush shake
seeds from its feathers

                          My body   my
thorned membrane   is there a story where
he   not us   tapers & snaps into a new
shape   Where we leave him   an uprooted
reed   to shrivel on the sun-parched bank

OBJECT LESSONS: AFTER SOLOMON J. SOLOMON'S *AJAX AND CASSANDRA*

Before her boyfriend pinned her
　　　to the parking lot & tore
　　　　　　her spandex skirt with his teeth, the girl
　　　had kissed coarse brine from his navel.

The preacher stresses this point
　　　as he reads newsclippings to rows
　　　　　　of children. Their silence, thick as gauze
　　　over a slit eye. *A creature bent toward*

her destruction he calls her. Just as Solomon
　　　paints Cassandra—straining over Ajax
　　　　　　toward Athena's altar, rainbowed pinions
　　　of light pressing her against her assailant.

She, a disciple of the gods,
　　　knows the lineage of women
　　　　　　Athena reshaped into fang & venom.
　　　Like Medusa, raped by Poseidon,

who watched her own scalp birth
　　　a nest of vipers, her skin mottle purple,
　　　　　　all her lovers zero to shale. Or
　　　Arachne, archivist of Zeus'

cruelest forms: indifferent swan,
　　　white bull, shaft of light. Only to have
　　　　　　this tapestry smash against her skull,
　　　her neck rake against a noose, her belly

bloat with silk. Still, Cassandra
    contorts herself toward
        an inevitable denial.
    An arc my arm mimics

as I extinguish cigarettes
    on my shoulders. A ritual
        begun after I split
    from my abuser—

to calm the daily contraction
    of the throat. To ward off
        desire. Harmed, what is left
    but our belief in further harm?

//

Burn marks. Fractured
    jaw. Congealed stain.
        The preacher lingers
    on each detail,

imagines the girl's body as a canvas
    of gashes & snares. This, the crux
        of his belief—
    pain transmuted into salvation,

as if he could milk
    thimblefuls of communion wine
        from her wounds. Solomon
    does not picture restoration

sprouting from terror, but beauty.
        False as a lilac in a jaguar's jaw.
                Which is why, with turpentine,
        he thins the oils weaving

Cassandra's dress. Fabric sheer &
        bunched below her waist. Hair
                an impressionistic fury of red.
        An erect nipple

where her mouth should be.
        Rape made fantasy.
                In reciting these stories, am I
        not guilty of the same? Our

bodies made aesthetic, digestible.
        Unwrapped hand & foot
                to see the welts, the plump grapes
        ready to pluck. The striptease

as I pry them from our flanks. *This is why*
        we should abandon this world & all the things
                thereof the preacher says. A sentiment
        gone unremarked when the girl sunders

her skull with buckshot
        six weeks after. Who can survive
                becoming allegory? Those details
        Solomon, too, strikes off the canvas—

Cassandra, in the end,
        welcomed the blades
                as they sang through her
        like a psalm. The way

I invited strangers'
       tongues, penises, & fists
              to abrade the wound. To crack
      it open & be conscious

in my surrender. *Grace*
     enough to wash even the musk
          of the unchaste, the preacher
     says in his benediction.

         Leave him his erasures. We fill,
or break, our own frames.

HIRAETH

Every girl must know her annunciation—
        This scarlet gown   floating over the bed as if worn
by air   is mine   After decades beneath
        its gaze   I finally pressed the neckline between

        my shoulderblades like an open mouth   The flesh
then   before the spirit   knew its vacancies
        Those goatheaded chimeras gnawing the absent
womb   One winter   I lactated wine & let

beasts ride me behind   the nativity until
        my hair grew wolfish as theirs   Now I shave
silver from my house key into tea for sleep   Now
        silence is my native tongue   & I can't come

        unless the capillaries threaten   to burst from
my neck   like tornado-stripped branches   *Reid*
        are you praying   my mother asks in a phone call
& somewhere an addict tars their aorta shut

Somewhere a rainstorm teeths open a monarch's
        wings   *Reid*   *are you eating*   & I swallow a pulped
psalter   only to retch up a moth made
        of papier-mâché   She chitters the unknowable

        hour of my rebirth before scattering
herself against the radiator   My Engineer
        my Lord   my Huntress—I have not been punished
enough for these negligences   When Your oracle

kisses my skin cystic   they'll be dressed in my best
        possible skeleton   The one grown in a timeline
where I held estradiol   between my teenaged
        teeth instead of men's sharkspine erections

        Where they name me *dyke* instead of *fag*   & the body's
holy as a salt circle   a bell ringing *sorrow*   *sorrow*
        When will the cocoon split empty   Please   honeycomb
my gut till lust turns to ulcer turns to—*sorrow*

SPINNERET GIRL AT THE END OF HER VISIONS

Overnight, the cobwebs latticing my rafters
reform with a new word torn

into their margins. Dragonflies, mid-
mating, gather as my mother's silhouette

at my doorstep, then disperse into
heat-warped ribbons of air. Revelator,

what use are these auspices now?
I sleep with a bundle of peonies in hand &

wake clasping a widow's unbodied
fingers. A radiovoice drones about

Christ lecturing the Samaritan woman
on the economics of pleasure, & I know

a syringe was the last thing to thumb the divot
of my partner's elbow. Please, let me go

unblessed. Let me dart into whatever mouth
swallowed her & mistake its warmth

for hers. When I at last tear these tarps
from the window, let light gnaw into

my eyes, the way nightcrawlers burrow
through a dead doe's sockets to find

brain, gutbraid, heart—that cherished
slurry of softs & salts & reds.

FUGUE WITH A PROCESSION OF VISITORS

First comes the memory of the pastor,
the family friend who once traced a goat's head
in the constellation of my freckles. *Son,* he warns,

you have the gift of visions. I leave hot water
running, let steam occlude every mirror. But come evening,
the serpent my father feared would seduce me

cinches a harness around my breasts,
biting my neck till I sigh *my darling,*
my provider, my Nyquil. By the third endearment,

the door splinters & a robber presses
his knife beneath my chin. He demands diamonds
but there are none left. As the blade enters,

I wake floating in the bathtub, a moth-winged angel
overhead. Outlined in her fur, the faces of friends
lost to madness. She extends

a palmful of Percocet but I deny it three times.
The fourth, I relent, weeping as each pill pupates,
turns into living, silver hairs. After flushing them down

the drain, I wipe a patch of the mirror clean, forgetting
my reflection. Stamen stalks erupt from her mouth
as the face, paper-like, peels back

into a corona of petals. My lily-headed double
raises her hand, scrawling a message in the filth-dusted glass:
We have rolled back the partition so you might

pass through. Fearful & sincere, I paint the mirror
white, a frost no bulb could sprout from. The body,
a bag of manna, gone stale & stolen from heaven.

THE INTERCESSION

This is the last
page in the Book of Cowards—

//

A heron with translucent skin
circles closer &
closer
to a lake, flash-frozen in midsummer.
Trout, caught breaching

the surface & gleaming
like nailheads, chant *you've given me up*
for dead. Each word gathers
as fog, as snowdrift, as pills
gone to little wakes of powder. I try

denying, but the lead plum between
my breasts ripens to
bursting.

In the pulp, a dollseye,
all glass & hollow & peeling paint.
At its center,
a miniature polaroid of me & Ann
on the northern bank of the Ohio—

//

[Unaware how light
  refracting from the river blotted
  out our faces. How
  the liquid, weightless things—
  photons, dope, sperm—would shear off
  our crowns. On the far shore,

  one woman tongues bits of poison ivy
  into her mouth as another
  watches.]

       //

The dollseye lolls
up as the heron
lands, scratching illegible text into the frost
at my feet. *Where else*

to look I ask, letting
the cellophane wings, the stickpin legs
clamp tight. She holds me

down till I understand the word
stinging & becoming my flesh: *stay, stay, stay.*

APOLOGIA

Beneath the milkweed
chandeliered with frost   a molted
husk of an asp observes its shadow

departing   None of us is meant to bear
adoration   Still the old hungers
surge   The veils woven

out of water   Each wedding band
smelted out of cold   Somewhere a goshawk
descends & a pair of women

dress themselves with wishbones in separate
rooms   On their windowsills
trilliums of ivy avert their faces from the sun

Silent & destined for more
silence

DEMETER: THE POEM AS MY MOTHER

after Paisley Rekdal's "Tiresias"

When my child confesses a longing
to reshape his body,
details the regimen of pills & syringes
for this purpose—
numbness vines along my spine.

The surgeries to come
recalling his seasons of illness—
those winters where
arrays of IVs & rubber hosing latched into him
like the talon of a hawk.
Hours spent wondering if surgeons
had discovered, at last,
why those rogue cells kept unlacing
the fabric of his colon.

On those sleepless nights, I'd remember
how I'd disregarded his complaints
of dull aches migrating across his gut.
How could you have known he reassures me
years later. Still, guilt builds
its nest in my body,

which flares now when I insist *you won't menstruate,
you won't be man or woman.*
My child inherited
this barbed tongue. Says *maybe that's the point,*
seethes *if we're measuring*

womanhood by shed linings, then
I'm as femme as they come. Even over

the phone, I know how hurt is dazzling
his face. That look of a fawn caught,
snapped-legged, in a bear trap.

This same shawl of panic
fell over him in the recovery ward
when I scrubbed flecks
of shit from under his thighs.
I had learned, by then, not to gasp
at how loosely skin hung
from his narrow hips, like the folds of a skirt.
Not to mention the tarnished
rubies of blood in the mess. Not to weep
until I left the room.

Death, like a spouse, has always curled
too closely to my child.

Once I found him in the bathroom peeling
skin from slashes on his wrists.
The shock of blood
startled him. Not out of fear—
but disappointment. As if he thought,
by shucking off flesh, he would uncover
a kinder body beneath. The whispered refrain
of *I'm sorry* hushed by the choir of cicadas
outside. Should I have recognized
their frantic re-bodying? How they can't
pair with one another without
first shedding their former shapes.

Should I have known there were sorrows
I could not unthread?

I'm learning to see my child anew—
copper hair washed out
with lavender dyes, lips roseate & burgeoning,
chokers cinching the Adam's apple.

Our conversations, a seasonal
collapse into prayer. A bounty of smoke.

My child begs *please, just once, call me
your daughter.* When my mouth opens, I hope
lilies will not wilt with frost, hope warmth
unspools from my breath.

SPINNERET GIRL IN THE FLOOD

Before sight, sound. Before the mad rush
of beetles & orb-weavers to our porch—

we heard the susurrus of legs whipping
against switchgrass, a loss kind enough

to announce its arrival. My brothers, turned toward
the simple faith in effort rewarded, began hammering

pests into mud with brick & steeltoe boot.
Each chitinous body cracking open

promised our home would not be both
mildewed & infested. Cruel jabs of hope.

Now, I search for reason where there is none—
The algae shellacking our basement. The crawdads peopling

our fields. The eight oily discs where
my eyes should've been. Impulsive believer,

I dress as a burnt Joan of Arc one day,
chew pentagrams into my lower lip

the next. But back when the silt-thick waters rose,
an answer, surer & more nameless, surfaced—

strands of black silk unwinding from the swollen
corners of my lips as I waded deeper.

PSALM AT THE END OF CICADA SEASON

Four months the swarm fattened the air
     with noise   with the wax membrane
of their wings   Now they've buried
     their young   silence opens its forceps

in the hollow of afternoon   Underfoot
     amber husks chime once more   Is it
wrong   god   to want a body
     emptied of memory   Here   rain

bloats an exposed beehive   A collarbone
     sinks   with the heft of its disappeared
necklace   & I've spent seventeen years
     translating the tymbals humming beneath

my tendon   muffled & promising
     as cricketsong heard underwater   My next
lover will call me her girl   watching
     as I molt dresses over doorknobs & bedposts

How do I explain the before—
     The prophets at the family barbecue
plucking tongue-pink coals
     from the pit   How I swallowed

each one   searing   ready to dissolve
     into its answer   Or the plainer history
stippled down my flank   Its pockmarks
     & half-filled ditches—

I've been a student of ecstasy so long   I've
          neglected what comes after   Those words
we bury into mattresses   trusting they will
          return as butter congealed on dinner plates

DRIFTERS

for k.p.

Do you remember when
salt first crisped your tongue?

The sharp blessing of it?

//

Between Seattle & Tampa, passenger jets empty
their bellies into the uncorrected

                                     mouths of mountains. A hunger gone

collective, so only an ocean could satiate us—
An all-hours seafood shack sizzling

                                     our names across the bay.

Lodes of grouper & rainbowed tails of shrimp
iridesce the grills.

                                     Below sightline—

Tanks of piled crabs. Their diffuse motions,
like fatty oils in a saucepan, slide.   Slow.   Slower.

                                     Then settle, unwitnessed.

//

What were we?

Children of floodplains & gulfs.
A displacement of water.

//

Beneath crackle of crustacean, breading against molar,
our histories, secrets skid across the table—

                    Mayflies skating the meniscus of creeks.

Outside, a hail of hard footfalls, knuckles against panes.
A man's threats crest like whitecaps

                    over a woman's protests.

We go static, cradling our own elbows
to stay their trembling—

                    The narratives moored

in my queer blood. Your woman blood.
The redshift of memory, of fear.

                    Silence falling like an accusation, I eat

the crabs, chitin
to pith, wishing I'd lay my hand

                    across your plate, palm upward—

A pale offering. A halved
lemon for want

      of the whole.

   //

  & what of the light fractaling the room?

     Its wordless bulbs greened with solitude,
     made voyeurs of us all.

NOTES & ACKNOWLEDGMENTS

In "Frontispiece," the line *of all things made new* pulls language from Isaiah 42:9 and Revelations 21:5.

"Aubade with Ball Gag's" epigraph comes from a 2006 article by Slavoj Žižek & his perceived notions of trans folks and their romantic lives, compared to the "perfect" union of (heterosexual) couples. His argument is an insistence that trans people are incapable of desire & romance. Also, the poem & its considerations owe much to Maggie Nelson's dissection of the article in *The Argonauts*.

The line *I opened for my beloved but she was gone* in "The Antlered Doe" pulls language from Song of Solomon 5:6.

"Cora, Bound to the Tree, Delivers Her Testimony" comes from the North Carolinian folktale of Cora the Witch, with details drawn from Episode 28 of the podcast *Lore*, "Making a Mark," by Aaron Mahnke.

"Of the Night's" line *name us a god who is a hooker* is indebted to Zoe Leonard's "I want a dyke for president…"

The following lines from "Object Lessons: After Solomon J. Solomon's *Ajax & Cassandra*" owe their language to Sylvia Plath's "Lady Lazarus:" *Unwrapped hand & foot / to see the welts, the plump grapes / ready to pluck. The striptease // as I pry them from our flanks.*

In "Drifters," the concept of *redshift* was first introduced to me by Kimberly Povloski, to whom the poem is dedicated and addressed. Whose voice and insight had such a hand in so many of these poems.

//

The author would like to thank the following publications & contests in which pieces of this manuscript first appeared, sometimes in earlier versions:

The Adroit Journal: "Psalm at the End of Cicada Season" and
    "Fugue with a Procession of Visitors"
Crazyhorse: "Cora, Bound to the Tree, Delivers Her Testimony"
Fugue: "When I Defend My Name in Court"
Hunger Mountain: "Aubade with Ball Gag" and "The Antlered Doe"
Indiana Review: "Demeter: The Poem as My Mother"
Malasaña: "Hiraeth"
Muzzle: "Spinneret Girl at the End of Her Visions"
New England Review: "Swanplume Boy's Epithalamium" and
    "Prayer: Syrinx"
Ninth Letter: "The Intercession"
Pleiades: "Frontispiece" (as "In Transition")
Vinyl Poetry and Prose: "Of the Night"

To the Board of Trustees of The Frost Place, the Creative Writing Program of Eastern Washington University, the Art + Design, Spanish & Gender, Women's, & Sexuality Studies Programs at Butler University , the Butler Summer Institute, the LitFUSE Conference for Pacific Northwestern Writers, & the Wisconsin Institute for Creative Writing for their generous support & their gifts of (re)creative time—

To Eduardo C. Corral, for selecting this manuscript, for your evocative poems which first convinced me to write, & for saying "poetry is the art of revision—"

To Ross White & Noah Stetzer & all the folks at Bull City Press for their kindness & brightness, under which *The Wishbone Dress* found shelter—

To Jennifer Thoreson for all her work—strange, wondrous, chimeric—which never fails to enrapture, but especially for her hybrid piece *Flora,* which feels so in concert with these poems. For gifting this book your brilliance and an otherworldly veil—

To my mentors—Alessandra Lynch, Jonathan Johnson, Christopher Howell—
who showed me this gift & encouraged me to pursue honesty above all else, at
all costs—

To my cohorts at Butler University & Eastern Washington University & Central
Washington University, who I wish I had space to name & whose friendships
have cultivated my writing, my activism, my hope—

To my family as we come together, forming our new common tongue with
equal parts uncertainity, curiosity, & joy for what it could contain, whose
understanding I hope I show gratitude for, at all times—

To my older brother, David, who saw me first, & whose unwavering support,
queer presence & affirmation, & passion for literature taught me what
sustenance there was in words—

To Hannah K., Molly N., Kate S., Emma L., Vic O., John L., Claire L.,
Kimberly P., Taylor K., Maura L., Lauren H., Chris M., Tracie F., Matt G.,
MaryLeauna C., Jay M., Victoria F., & Alia B., whose warmth & friendship has
sustained me through the most tumultuous & most radiant days. Who've, in a
word, kept me alive—

& to A., I miss you, dearly, & hope wherever & whatever circle you're in is kind,
listens to your song—

This book, the shawl it weaves, is yours, and has always been.

ABOUT THE AUTHOR

Cassandra J. Bruner, born and raised in Indiana, earned her MFA in poetry from Eastern Washington University. Recipient of the 2019-2020 Jay C. and Ruth Halls Fellowship from the Wisconsin Institute of Creative Writing, she has also been the finalist for the 2018 *Black Warrior Review* Nonfiction Contest & the 2019 *Third Coast* Poetry Contest. A transfeminine poet and essayist, their writing has appeared in *The Adroit Journal*, *Black Warrior Review*, *Crazyhorse*, *Malasaña*, *New England Review*, *Third Coast*, and elsewhere.

ABOUT THE FROST PLACE CHAPBOOK COMPETITION

The Frost Place is a nonprofit educational center for poetry and the arts based at Robert Frost's old homestead, which is owned by the Town of Franconia, New Hampshire. In 1976, a group of Franconia residents, led by David Schaffer and Evangeline Machlin, persuaded the Franconia town meeting to approve the purchase of the farmhouse where Robert Frost and his family lived full-time from 1915 to 1920 and spent nineteen summers. A board of trustees was given responsibility for management of the house and its associated programs, which now include several conferences and seminars, readings, a museum located in the Frost farmhouse, and yearly fellowships for emerging American poets.

The Frost Place Chapbook Competition awards an annual prize to a chapbook of poems. In addition to publication of the collection by Bull City Press, the winning author receives a fellowship to The Frost Place Poetry Seminar, a cash prize, and week-long residency to live and write in The Frost Place farmhouse.

2019   Cassandra J. Bruner, *The Wishbone Dress*
            SELECTED BY EDUARDO C. CORRAL

2018   Yuki Tanaka, *Séance in Daylight*
            SELECTED BY SANDRA LIM

2017   Conor Bracken, *Henry Kissinger, Mon Amour*
            SELECTED BY DIANE SEUSS

2016   Tiana Clark, *Equilibrium*
            SELECTED BY AFAA MICHAEL WEAVER

2015   Anders Carlson-Wee, *Dynamite*
            SELECTED BY JENNIFER GROTZ

2014   Lisa Gluskin Stonestreet, *The Greenhouse*
            SELECTED BY DAVID BAKER

2013   Jill Osier, *Should Our Undoing Come Down Upon Us White*
            SELECTED BY PATRICK DONNELLY